LARN YARSEL E

Thass a proper

To my family who have
encouraged my efforts at
writing

Larn Yarsel Essex

Words by
Richard Thomas

Illustrations by
Gerry Madder-Smith

NOSTALGIA
Publications

TOFTWOOD · DEREHAM · NORFOLK

Originally Published by:
NOSTALGIA PUBLICATIONS

First Impression 1999

Reprinted June 2000 by:
JOHN NICKALLS
Oak Farm Bungalow, Suton,
Wymondham, Norfolk NR18 9SH

ISBN 0 947630 27 9

Design and Typesetting:
NOSTALGIA PUBLICATIONS

Printed by:
BARNWELL'S PRINT LTD.
Penfold Street, Aylsham, Norfolk NR11 6ET

Contents

The deepest Essex few explore
Where steepest thatch is sunk in flowers
And out of elm and sycamore
Rise flinty fifteenth century towers

Acknowledgements

Thank you to Terry Davy for giving me the chance and the encouragement to write this book about Essex. I also want to pay tribute to Gerry Madder-Smith for his drawings; you'll see how they bring the text to life. I am indebted to a number of people, too numerous to mention specifically, who have let me tap into their memories and have taken me back to half forgotten words and sayings from the old Essex that is slipping away, although, I particularly want to thank Ron White who has helped me here. My mother has been more than helpful in getting her friends to recall names of flowers, birds and the old Essex food as well as listing all the superstitions and prohibitions that ruled the lives of most of us for our earlier years, Jill who gave me the recipe for the bacon pudding must be mentioned.

I thank John Murray, the publishers of John Betjeman's collected poems for the quote from Essex, Bob Napp who provided a family photograph for the front cover and Wayne who helped put it together.

A vicar was surprised to meet one of his young Sunday School pupils driving a large cow along a country lane.

"Morning, Lucy, why are you not in Sunday School?"

"Please, sar, oim a'takin' Daisy ter be bulled."

"Couldn't your father do that?"

"Oh no, sar … That hev ter be a bull!"

Introduction

I came to start this from reading *Larn Yarself Silly Suffolk* by David Woodward. I wrote to him about the overlap between words and sayings that I had known and used years ago in mid Essex and those from Suffolk and, lo and behold, Terry Davy wrote to me asking if I would like to do the same for Essex. I said I would have a go and this is the result.

In the book, I look at the Essex dialect as I recall it in mid Essex and try to give a few pointers as to how it might be spoken, as well as a dictionary of the words I could find still in use or which I could trace as having been used in living memory.

Apart from my own recollections, my sources are friends, family and local contacts, which I have backed up from the Essex Dialect Dictionary, published in 1920, some of the works of S. L. Bensusan, C. H. Warren and research done on the use of local words in the 1960s. For the place names I have had recourse to the Place Names of Essex, published in 1936 which remains the authority on the County.

I have also recorded some of the superstitions I remember as a child here and I have suggested some places and things which are both worth seeing and, more, worth going to see because they are unique to Essex. Inevitably these are selective and personal but I hope that as a minimum they awaken an interest in seeing what the County has to offer.

In recent years, Essex has had a bad press. The county has become known for Essex man and Essex girl jokes. I'm afraid you'll find none of them here. This is about the other Essex, the rural county, as it was after the war and as it still is in the North and away from the main roads and the railways. The pace of life is slower and steadier; some of the old country values still hold and you can still hear the rhythm and flow of the Essex dialect.

I used a verse written by the late Sir John Betjeman at the front of this book and I make no apology for repeating it here as, in my view, it comes closer than anything else that I have read to expressing the essence of Essex as it still is in the remote rural corners:-

The deepest Essex few explore
Where steepest thatch is sunk in flowers
And out of elm and sycamore
Rise flinty fifteenth-century towers

From A Few Late Chrysanthemums (1954).

This Essex can still be found, although the elms have gone with Dutch Elm Disease and many of the hedgerows have been grubbed up to form prairies. The rest of the poem will pay reading.

The vast influx of people to Essex over the last 50 years has turned much of a still rural county into suburbia. Some of the incomers were transplanted from London after the war into the new towns of Harlow and Basildon or to overspill estates attached to existing small towns like Witham. Most came when the railways were modernised and travel into London became easy and relatively convenient.

They were generally seen as foreigners and, to be honest, never belonged in village life. The old Essex people tended to opt out and leave things like the Parish Council in the hands of the newcomers as Essex people rarely push themselves forward. Complaints about church bells, bonfires and animal smells and noises, mud on the roads and being stuck behind combines and tractors highlighted and still highlight the gulf between old and new.

It's wrong to dwell on the past. It's gone with the elm trees and, although we might mourn what has been lost, it is lost and can't be resurrected. I hope however that this book will jog some memories of those who spoke Essex once but have perhaps dropped it or let it go out of memory and it might attract some who have migrated here and who would like to know more about some of the old words and the way of life that these words reflected.

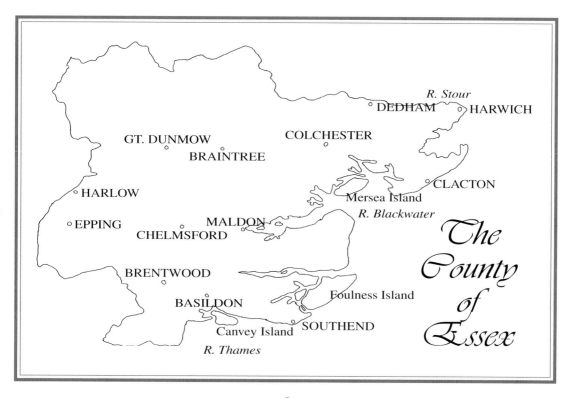

R. Stour

DEDHAM HARWICH

GT. DUNMOW COLCHESTER

BRAINTREE

CLACTON

HARLOW Mersea Island

R. Blackwater

EPPING MALDON

CHELMSFORD

BRENTWOOD

BASILDON Foulness Island

Canvey Island SOUTHEND

R. Thames

The County of Essex

Quiet Corner of Galleywood

Section One

The Essex
Dialect

The ancient verger acted as guide for a tour of the village church, and gave a most detailed history of the building.

When he had finished he invited the visitors to place a donation on the collection plate near the door. They all did so, except for one well-heeled gentleman in a tweed suit.

As the party boarded their bus, the verger called to the man who had failed to make a contribution:

"Scuse me bor, but if yew should find yew hent got yer wallet when yer git hoom, jist yer remember yer dint tek it out har!"

The Essex dialect is probably dying, if not dead, in most of the South of the County from Chelmsford down to the Thames and across to Epping. It can still be heard amongst the older people in the villages there, but a strangulated London accent, which uses fewer letters than any other I have ever heard (no Hs, few Ts, Th. becoming F, R merging into W, A and E colliding and so on), has taken over. But go north and east of Chelmsford, go into the country areas and particularly go to Colchester and there, in a large town, you can still hear Essex spoken by most people, both as a dialect and using the Essex accent, which is of course how the dialect is spoken.

This book tries to recall some of the old words, sayings and ways of speaking as a record of a way of life which is fast disappearing under the sophistication of television, computers and the modern world, not to mention bricks, concrete and well laid out lawns instead of vegetable gardens lovingly tended with a few flowers for the house.

The dictionary cites a number of the old words that have dropped out of use with the move from the land and the mechanisation of farming. Nowadays, where once twenty or thirty worked, a farm might employ two or three men, (and they are likely to be the farmer's sons), so the weakening of the dialect is partly a product of this.

The Essex dialect reflects, admittedly distantly, the language of one of the great poems in Old English - the Battle of Maldon. This poem commemorates, even celebrates the death of Byrhtnoth, a Saxon Earl, in a battle against the Danes. Some of the language used is stirring even now:-

The spirit must be the firmer, the heart the bolder,

Courage must be the greater as our strength diminishes.

Or, in old English

Hige sceal the hearda, heorte the cenre
mod sceal the mare the ure maegen lytlao

(from D Scragg's translation in the Battle of Maldon, Blackwell, 1991)

Much of the poem is lost but it stands as one of the earliest links between the Anglo-Saxon past and the present language. The root of current English is Old English and in light of the residual words and dialect structure of the old way of speaking in Essex, it is fair to draw the parallel. The battle itself took place at the causeway to Northey island to the east of Maldon. The island is normally private but it is open to the public once a year in summer and this is well worth looking out for as a unique opportunity to visit a secluded place. But go to the marshes on the Blackwater, near Maldon, if you can in winter when the nights are drawing in and the mist is rising, and you can still get some of the atmosphere of an ancient battlefield, where stirring deeds were done and heroism was celebrated in old verse and fine words.

A young lad went into the village shop just before closing time on Saturday evening.

"Toilet roll, please mister."

The shopkeeper took one down from the shelf and handed it to the boy, and gave him the change from half-a-crown.

First thing Monday morning the lad was back in the shop with the toilet roll under his arm.

"Mum says kin yer tek that back cos tha cumpany dint cum!"

Maldon

A dialect is a true variety of a language with its own rules of spelling and grammar and its own vocabulary, combining words which have disappeared from standard English with the words that have been in use locally for many generations and which never were used anywhere else. Often slang words catch on and become part of normal use - rhyming slang for cockneys is a good example.

Dialect stems from the oral tradition where words and memory were entwined. This was a necessary way of life before reading and writing became general. People had to commit what was important to them to memory otherwise it would be lost.

Yet now, the visual message is so strong and global that we risk losing our oral heritage to a global international culture. In addition, the strength and vitality of urban life is overshadowing what used to be the diversity of village life. People may be as much swayed in fashions of speech as they are in what they wear.

As I write this, I have been reading press reports that Glaswegians and Liverpudlians are beginning to sound like Londoners, using what is called Estuary English, from North Kent and South Essex; people in South Wales are adopting a Birmingham twang, and this is on top of the international, transatlantic slang that is generally adopted by the young which their elders try to follow and make fools of themselves in so doing.

Memory was essential in passing down family history, folklore and customs, superstitions and how work was done. It explained how and why things happened. Old people were reluctant to put things down on paper as it might tie them down and so their memories were well trained and used. They

Lock Keepers
Cottage
Dedham

were also wonderfully inventive in making up new words or adapting old ones for new uses.

Stories were handed down across the years. People delighted in hearing about others, both dead and alive, and many reputations grew or were destroyed in the stories told around pub fires and amongst the women. Tales were handed down within families as well; contrary and opputarious (difficult) relations were known to generations long after they had died. It's strange to think that in older days people could well have been better remembered perhaps than they are now with the photographs and videos we all use. In Suffolk, George Ewart Briggs has recorded the oral tradition which pervades much of Suffolk still. The same traditions apply in Essex but perhaps less strongly and on a narrower basis. The knack and love of story telling is less important than it was. Nowadays, almost everyone can read and write and there isn't the reluctance on the part of country people to commit themselves by writing and, more, by signing anything. The mass media and especially television have crowded out the old ways and people now rely on the television as a source of conversation rather than the doings of their neighbours. It is also probably the case that villages have grown less close knit with their expansion and through the increase in second homes in rural areas.

Old spoken Essex was a true dialect as it had its own grammar, vocabulary and pronunciation. It was and is close to Suffolk and there are a number of similar words; there are also considerable differences. Like Suffolk, it was strong in the oral tradition where people used their memories and everything was handed down from generation to generation. Words were coined to meet new situations and as time went on they became enshrined in tradition. Because the main work in the county was farming, much of spoken Essex related to that. Most of the other words and sayings came from domestic activity and from names of birds, animals and plants.

Learn and learning are used generally in Essex for teach and teaching. In addition, learning means education. The word learn goes back to the Old English lieran which means teach and it is interesting to note that, in modern German, lehren means to teach. So an Essex father might say to his son, "I'll larn you how ter do that boy." This might be to help him or to punish him for a wrongdoing. Whichever is the case, it takes the use of learn in Essex right back to its Germanic roots.

Many people still say they haven't time for learning which can also mean books and papers. They'll buy a paper for the gays (pictures) but reading is not seen as a normal activity but, more usually, as a last resort - there are generally far more important things to do in the garden than to waste time reading.

Hatfield Forest

Ulting Church

The Essex Dialect

The grammar of spoken Essex is easy. Present and past tenses are close so "I see that" is both I am seeing that and I have seen it. Past tenses can also come in the form of "I shewd him that" from show in the present, for example. Emphasis is laid on sentences through auxiliaries like "I am now comin'"; "I hev sin it"; "I will do that"; "I unt goo". The use of "it"is very limited in Essex, "that" is more generally spoken instead.

Pronouncing Essex is difficult. We've all heard actors (and comedians) trying to talk like us and it's rare to hear it spoken correctly. Most end up talking mummerset (the all purpose stage rural accent).

The quickest test for someone's ability to speak Essex is to listen if they drop their hs; if they do, they are not speaking with the Essex accent however many Essex words they might use.

The other obvious sign is that Essex speakers have trouble with diphthongs - they are not a normal part of speech so, school is skoowull; road is rooad; town is towun; train is trayun and of course the river Stour is the Stoower and so on.

So, if yer wanter speak crectly, the two things yer do are don't drop yer hs and moind yer don't use yer diphthongs.

Consonants are now generally the same as in Standard English - although for example, at one stage v was often pronounced as a w - but the vowel sounds do differ:

A often becomes lengthened into an aar sound;

E can become a in some words - arth for earth for example; ew is almost always pronounced oo so few becomes foo.

I often turns into e, so pick is spoken as peck, or into oi so moine replaces mine;

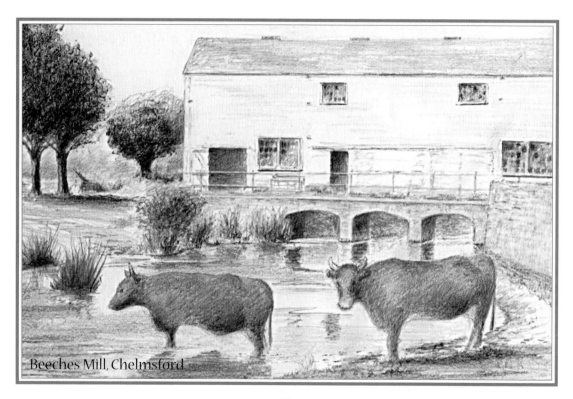

Beeches Mill, Chelmsford

O is often like oo as in poost office, u in furriner and er as in yeller, do is pronounced as to near to doe as you can get;

U, as in tulip/duke, is always pronounced oo as in toolip and dook.

Essex speakers always both stress and draw out the first syllable of long words and then chop off the rest - listen to how place-names are pronounced and you'll start to get the idea. Next, you have to sing song a bit up and down the scale; not as much as in Welsh but you need a good ear for the rhythm of spoken Essex. This needs a lot of practice, preferably in private, unless your family are very understanding and not given to mockery. Finally, if you can gradually raise the pitch of your voice towards the end of a sentence as if you're asking a question, then you will be close to mastering Essex as she is spoke.

An important feature is the speed of speech. As a generalisation, the women tend to speak slower than the men and, although some of the older men do speak very slowly; others talk quickly, even gabble, so someone unfamiliar with Essex can be hard put to understand a single word, let alone catch the gist of what is being said.

Many Essex people have deliberately tried to lose their accent because to an unsympathetic listener, the speaker will sound rustic and unsophisticated. It is also the case that the schools tried to teach us how to speak properly in elocution classes and this added to the pressure to lose the way we talked. A vicious circle has set in whereby the accent is less often used and becomes less familiar and as such sounds strange, and so it is used less and becomes less normal and is in turn used less and so on. The vitality of both the London accent and its own dialect also have a lot to do with the decline of our own accent.

As well as the accent and dialect being quite difficult to speak, in Essex people can very often be quite off-putting to someone used to more outgoing people. If you're invited in to someone's house, it may not be with a welcome mat and hail fellow well met but on the lines of "I suppose you'd better come in then, if you like". That is a real welcome as hospitality is only given once barriers come down so, if you get invited 'round to mine', feel honoured and accept it.

If you ask someone from Essex if they can help you, again you may be surprised to hear what you can take to be a very grudging reply. That is however, just Essex caution which in part goes back to the times when farm hands were unwilling to give too much, lest advantage was taken.

In the same way, people may not be very direct when approaching you. Partly this is native caution and not wishing to appear too forward but also it is a reflection that Essex can be a very private county where many are reluctant to intrude, although this is in strong conflict with the wish to learn all that can be known about a new presence in the village. This may mean that although no direct question will be asked, in conversation, statements will be made and the response assessed carefully before onward transmission round the grape vine.

A piece of advice is not to try to talk Essex in front of Essex people unless you are sure you can. If you make a mess of it, you'll be both very subtly cut off as a smart foreigner and laughed at behind your back for as long as you're around and then some.

A man knocked on the farmhouse door. When the farmer answered the man said,"I am dreadfully sorry, but I have just ran over your cockerel. However, you'll be pleased to hear that I would like to replace it."

The farmer smiled, and replied:"Well, I dunt know how yer'll mek out, but best yer goo round the back where the hins are!"

The Essex Dialect   THE DOS AND DONTS

You won't be around the older Essex people long before you hear how much they use the word do. It means the normal activity in English, as you might expect. But there is a number of extra ways in which do and don't are used by Essex people. They might double as (and here we have to get a bit technical) the imperative - "Do yer get the paper booy, I want to scan the gays afore I goo out". They can mean if and if not - the conditional "Do you keep on boy you'll feel my hand.". Do is a way of emphasising a feeling as in "Do gal, I am wholly whacked".

The story is told of a farmhand who sent the boy to fetch something from the barn. He came back saying it wasn't there. The old man said "Thass a rum un. Do that don't that did."

Windmill at Aythorpe Roding

Chelmer Park, Galleywood

Section Two

An Essex Miscellany

George was showing an American tourist round the village.

"Thas our church … took nigh on twenty year ter build years ago."

"Waal," drawled the American. "guess in Texas we could erect one in five."

George then pointed out the village hall.

What about that there, then? Took only nine month ter build."

"Waal," said the American, "guess back home we can errect a hall like that in six months."

They turned the corner and there stood the new council school, with sports hall and playing fields.

"Say, buddy, what's that building then?"

"Dunno" said George, "thet wunt there when I cum ter wark this mornin'!"

Essex Place Names

Towards the end of the Roman occupation, what became England began to experience the migration of Germanic peoples. The Saxons moved early into Essex and became the East Saxons with their own kingdom, which included London, Middlesex and parts of Hertfordshire.

The reasons for the movement of people across from what is now Germany are not clearly understood but the fort at Othona at Bradwell-Juxta-Mare was one of the forts of the Saxon shore built in late Roman times to guard against the invaders from the east. The fort is now very difficult to find because of coastal erosion and because much of its building material was used to good effect in St Peter's on the Wall. This is the earliest Saxon church in Essex and is essential visiting for anyone interested in history and atmosphere, situated as it is away from the village looking out to sea where access would be easier than by land.

Essex place names give two main indications of this early settlement by the Saxons. Firstly, the word 'ge', from old English meaning a tribal group, modern German 'gau', is a sign of a family or small tribal grouping and for example both the areas round Ingatestone and the Roothings, as well as Vange, seem from recent research to have settled in this way.

The tribe around Ingatestone were the gingas and they gave their name to the settlements from Margaretting across to Warley. One of the oddest of the lot is an older name for what is now Buttsbury - Ginges Joyberd Laundry; the latter two parts were the names of the Norman feudal overlords who held the land. Buttsbury now means Botolph's pear tree - not nearly as interesting as its earlier

Margaretting

name! The other indication is the number of places that have pagan elements in their names such as:- Thundersley, Weeley, Broxted, Thurstaple (the hundred between Maldon and the Tolleshunts/Mersea) and Thunderlow the lost hundred in North Essex.

The Essex people were known to have stayed pagan for longer than any others in the Anglo-Saxon world and, at one stage, recanted their Christianity during a plague. Indeed there was a time when the East Saxon Kingdom had joint kings, one was Christian and the other was pagan. Maybe this was taking insurance a bit too far.

In contrast to Suffolk, the place names show that Essex was very much under the feudal yoke and the village names still strongly reflect this with the old Anglo-Saxon name having the Norman lord's name as a suffix - the Layers (Breton, Marney and de la Haye) and the Tolleshunts (D'Arcy, Major and Knights) - are good examples of this. In Suffolk, the likelihood is that these villages would have had saints names differentiating them.

Interestingly, some names confirm that a lot of the older, pre Saxon, inhabitants remained - for example, Walden means dene/valley of the foreigners - the Welsh in other words. It has been said that this accounts for the fact that many Essex people are darker haired than their neighbours in Suffolk and Norfolk although, as far as I know, this has never been tested by taking blood samples. Some older pre Saxon names survive, generally in river names such as the Pant and the Stour but also, for example, in some settlement names such as Dovercourt which contains a Celtic root word for water, douvr, that has become dwr in modern Welsh.

Essex also has some unusual names for its villages, ends and tyes. Some are quite pretty like Gay Bowers, Good Easter and Mellow Purgess; many are odd, even comical, like Cock Clarks, Nipsells Rayment, Steeple Bumpstead, Snoreham and Twitty Fee. Some are perhaps strange to foreign ears like Fobbing, Messing, Mucking, Vange, Pitsea, and especially Shellow Bowells, not to mention Ugley with its famous Women's Institute.

"Old Moot", Castle Headingham

A number of explanations of names are enshrined in tradition like Gore Pit at Feering where Boadicea or Boudicca (whichever you prefer) was supposed to have massacred a tidy few (or several) Romans. Unfortunately, there is a rational definition of it as Gorr pit meaning a pit full of muck. My own home village of Galleywood was always defined literally as the place where wood for galleys was obtained, and this was usually good enough for a prize in the local paper's competition for children of 'What does my village name mean?'. It actually means a tax or tribute wood.

Some time ago, someone put together an old rhyme of Essex names:

Willingale Doe and Willingale Spain,
Bulvan and Bobbingworth, Colne Engaine,
Wenden Lofts, Beamont cum Moze, Bung
 Row,
Gestingthorpe, Ugley and Fingringhoe:
Helions Bumpstead and Mountnessing,
Bottle End, Tolleshunt D'Arcy, Messing,
Islands of Canvey, Foulness, Potton,
Stondon Massey and Belchamp Otton:
Ingrave and Inworth and Kedington,
Shellow Bowells, Ulting and Kelvedon;
Margaret Roothing and Manningtree -
The bolder you sound 'em the better they
 be.

This is a fitting way to keep some of the more memorable place names firmly in your mind.

Remember that, when you pronounce an Essex name, you draw out the first syllable and chop off the rest so Chelmsford becomes Chelllmsfd (Chimsford if you're from Ford End), Maldon, Maawldn (but Malldon if you're from Maldon), and so on. In addition, wherever possible, Essex people will be economical with names so South Woodham Ferrers is always Woodham, Great Baddow is Baddow (pronounced Badder) but Little Baddow keeps its describer and this is the case all over where there are Greats and Littles and where one place has become more important than others with the same root name.

Essex and Time

It is not generally known (outside the County that is) that Essex people are philosophers and cosmologists who, long before Einstein, and Stephen Hawking, had developed the idea of time as a wholly elastic concept which could be stretched at will to range from absolute immediacy to a complete sense of infinity - from here to eternity as it were.

Time in Essex is also seen as being the servant of man which has to be both relative and capable of being slowed to the pace which is right for the situation and quickened up if that suited the user's own convenience (and not that of anyone he was working for).

Being economical of speech, and, having a well developed sense of the importance of the idea, Essex people can encapsulate all this in one word - directly, pronounced dreckly. It has taken the great minds from foreign parts (Cambridge and beyond into the sheers, wherever they might be) books full of learning to explain the same thing, but them're wonderful sharp ent they?

Directly means anything from "I'll do it now" right through to "I tell master I'll do that directly but, do he reckon he'll see that done, do he'll be dead first". If pushed to an explanation, some may be prepared to allow that directly actually means "directly I get round to it", but this skates over the real depth of meaning.

Other people, such as the Spanish, have similar expressions - manana for example - but it should be obvious that directly is a far more useful word since manana does convey a specific time (albeit that tomorrow never comes) whereas directly is absolutely vague and the user can never be pinned down. It is said that there is no word in Irish for manana because it implies too much haste. In that case, Essex people can commend directly to the people of Ireland as meeting all their requirements for an absence of haste as well as the extremely useful extra attributes of ambiguity and imprecision.

In the same way, many Essex people have learnt how to defy the laws of gravity. Have you seen how slowly many of them can ride a bike? But that's another story.

Old Pillar Box at Margaretting Tye

Superstitions and Sayings

Essex people had and still have a host of superstitions and prohibitions to guide their lives. Some are no doubt confined to the older members of the community nowadays but scratch someone from Essex and you will find that they can reel off a great list of things that they learnt as children, of which even now they are still aware and half consciously follow and believe.

This list is not exhaustive. It is gathered from my own childhood and supplemented by friends' recollections.

- You should always leave a house by the same door as the one you used coming in.
- A dead snake won't lose its poison until the sun goes down (This is not so strange as it appears. Research in the USA has found that a rattle snake's poison can still take effect an hour after the snake is dead).
- You should always wear something new at Easter.
- May in the house is bad luck.
- Elder is as well, because it was believed to have been the wood the cross was made from and its use indoors and, especially, as firewood was bad luck.
- A new moon seen through glass was bad luck but it was averted if you could turn over the coins in your pocket.
- Crossed knives meant bad luck.
- If a child had a birth mark it inevitably meant that the mother has been frightened by something during pregnancy or for example, a strawberry mark meant she had overindulged in strawberries when pregnant.
- Never open an umbrella indoors.
- Never cross on the stairs.
- Never help anyone to salt.

The River Roding at Passingford Bridge

- Never put boots and shoes on a table.
- Never walk under a ladder.
- Rooks nesting low in trees mean a bad summer.
- If salt is spilt, throw a pinch over your left shoulder.
- Always turn mirrors and pictures to the wall during a thunder storm .
- If mourners at a funeral walked in threes, another death would follow.
- Never fail to pick up a pin:

See a pin and pick it up
And all the day you'll have good luck

See a pin and let it lie
Before the evening you will cry

- See an ambulance and say "Touch your collar, be a scholar, never catch a fever".
- Magpies - one for sorrow, two for joy, three for a girl and four for a boy. You could avert the bad luck at seeing a single magpie by addressing it politely and enquiring of its well being.
- Killing a beetle will bring rain.

- Killing a spider is unlucky - If you wish to live and thrive, let the spider run alive.
- The small spiders were always money spiders and one on you was a sign of money or good luck coming to you.
- If a lump of coal falls out of the fire it means luck.
- A picture falling off the wall means a death.
- Never pick up someone's gloves or bad luck will follow.
- Thirteen moons in a year mean a wet year.
- Christmas decorations went up on Christmas Eve and came down on Twelfth Night. (What a contrast to today!)
- If you gave someone a purse, it had to have a bit of cash in it or the purse would always be empty.
- You never gave knives, scissors or shears as presents for fear friendship would be cut.

It's a wonder how anyone managed to do anything with all these worrying rules to follow.

An old children's counting game to eliminate the odd one out is recorded by C. H. Warren:

Deena,dina, deena, dus,
Cattla, weena, wina, wus
Spit, spot, must be done,
Twiddlum, twaddlleum, twenty one,
O-u-t spells out.

There is a theory that this and similar rhymes have a very long history in that they were used to count out sacrificial victims in pagan times.

The Old Admiral Rouse, Galleywood

Some Essex People

Like most counties, Essex has some famous people who have been born, lived, died and been buried here. Some have lived all their lives here, others have come to be buried. I want to mention a few of the (to me) more interesting people without listing everyone whom I can trace that has some tie with Essex.

Setting aside Old King Coel from Colchester (Cymbeline in Shakespeare), the most elevated of these are King Harold who was buried at Waltham Abbey after his death at the Battle of Hastings and Anne Boleyn whose head is rumoured to lie in East Horndon Church. The Boleyns were an Essex family with manors at Rochford and Boreham. She is supposed to haunt New Hall in Boreham, which was her father's house until Henry VIII seized it after her execution, with her head tucked underneath her arm, as the song goes. New Hall is now a girls school and I have heard no recent reports of the late Queen's activities. Queen Boadicea or Boudicca just passed through the county, burning Colchester and massacring the inhabitants, on her way from Norfolk to London and, by popular account, slaughtering a Roman Legion at Gore Pit near Kelvedon.

Apart from Queen Elizabeth the First's speech to the troops at Tilbury, Essex connections with royalty become sparse until the late nineteenth century when the Prince of Wales, later King Edward VII paid frequent visits to Easton Court to see his close friend, Daisy Maynard, the Countess of Warwick.

The County has produced a number of less than respectable characters in its history - some of noble birth others humbly born. Richard Rich who became a Knight and then a Lord, finishing as Lord Chancellor of England is buried at Felstead where he founded the school.

Before then, he is notable as the man who betrayed Sir Thomas More by perjuring himself through inventing statements he claimed were made by Sir Thomas, in the same way as he had done for Bishop Fisher. He went on to help with the fall of the next Lord Chancellor, Thomas Cromwell, and, for the rest of his days, betrayed his friends to save his skin, becoming very wealthy in the process. He proclaimed the accession of Lady Jane Grey and then rode to Essex to proclaim Mary Tudor as Queen. As well as founding Felstead school, he built the magnificent Tudor house at Leez Priory, which needless to say he acquired through the dissolution of the monasteries. Alas for morality, loyalty and the wages of sin, he prospered and died in his bed at a good age.

A similar character was Thomas Howard, Earl of Suffolk and Lord Treasurer of England who embezzled large sums of money during his term of office. It might be argued that there was an unintended benefit in that he used much of the money (£200,000) to good effect in building Audley End but in the end, fraud is still fraud. The house itself is only a shadow of what he actually built with three of the four sides demolished leaving only the west block, but it is still well worth seeing, with Capability Brown's parkland. When he first saw Audley End, King James VI and I is said to have remarked "It is too much for a king but it might do very well for a Lord Treasurer".

The village of Hempstead is notable for two contrasting figures - William Harvey, who discovered the circulation of blood and Dick Turpin. William Harvey was the court physician who accompanied Charles I throughout the Civil War. He had been lecturer in anatomy and surgery at the College of Physicians when he made his discovery but its later publication and his royalist connections caused some hostility to him and he retired to Essex where he died in 1657. Dick Turpin was born in 1706 in the village inn, was apprenticed to a butcher and then took to rustling cattle, whether to cut out the middle man or simply for the fun of it is not known. When things got too hot for him, he fled to South Essex where

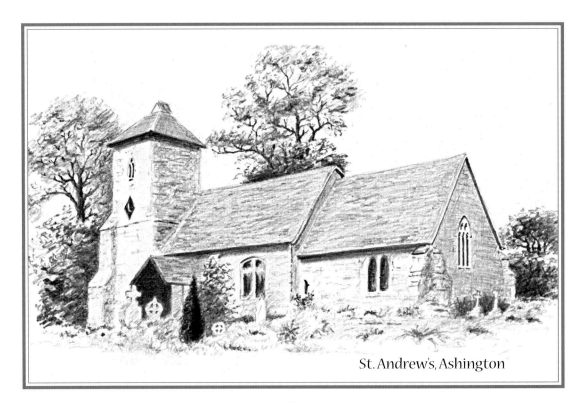

St. Andrew's, Ashington

he took up smuggling in and around Rochford and Dengie Hundreds. From there he seems to have gravitated to highway robbery and incidental murders in Epping Forest. Unfortunately, the romance of his ride to York on Black Bess is just that and, although he was hanged there for horse stealing in 1739, his ride to York was not the heroic dash of fiction. He had fled north from Essex because he had allegedly accidentally shot and killed one of his gang, Tom King. Black Bess was his horse so that part at least is true.

Manningtree in the north east was where one of the nastiest pieces of work in Essex history lived. Matthew Hopkins, the Witch Finder General, lived here in the mid seventeenth century and led the pursuit of witches in much of the East of England. There was a hysteria about witch craft at that time, partly brought about by King James' own views which were, for him, unusually credulous, although he had apparently been the target of witches when sailing back from Denmark with his new Queen Anne so it can be reasonably said that he might have some justification for his views. Matthew Hopkins came to a bad end when he was accused of witchcraft himself and put to death. I mention a bit more about witchcraft below on Canewdon.

The seventeenth century philosopher John Locke lived the last years of his life at Little Laver and is buried there. William Byrd, whose church music and madrigals delight still, lived, probably died and was buried at Stondon Massey although there is no trace of his grave. As a Catholic he would have been seen at that time as a traitor and hence had to live outside the establishment. Byrd's teacher, Thomas Tallis was the organist at Waltham Abbey. Other composers who were associated with Essex for a while were Gustav Holst who lived at Thaxted after the First World War and Armstrong Gibbs at Danbury.

Black Notley can boast of John Ray who was born in 1628 and died back in his village in 1705 and lies there still. He was a butcher's son who went to Cambridge, became a lecturer in Greek and Maths and took holy orders. The changing religious times forced him out and he devoted the rest of his life to natural history, completing his great work, the History of Plants just before his death. He established the first classification of natural life and can be said to have used scientific method in his work using observation and thorough experimentation to reach his conclusions.

Look at a map of New England in the USA and you can find Chelmsford, Danbury, Billericay and a number of other Essex place names. This is because many Essex people emigrated in the 17th century to follow their puritan religion which was out of favour at home. Billericay has strong links with the Mayflower as a Billericay man, Christopher Martin, was one of the original party who came to England in 1619 from Holland to charter and provision the ship. He was appointed the Governor of the ship in which sailed three others from Billericay but, unfortunately, neither he nor his wife survived the first winter in America. Other Essex people followed them to exercise their right to their own beliefs; these included the Washingtons from Purleigh in 1657, and, it is claimed, the Bushes from Messing. Essex had been an area where the Protestant religion and dissent from the established church had been strong from the early 16th century. Indeed, Essex was second only to London in the number of people burnt at the stake for their religion in Mary Tudor's reign.

Essex men participated in the Peasants Revolt from the south of the county. Jack Straw is associated with Fobbing on the Thames and the leaders are commemorated there and in what used to be Wat Tyler Park in Basildon. It ended in tears with the leaders betrayed by King Richard II, Jack Straw being executed with the usual barbarity and their followers massacred near Billericay. Essex is also associated with John Ball whose ideas influenced the rebels. Among his writings is:

When Adam delved and Eve span,
Who was then the gentleman?

John Ball was executed in 1381 along with the other leaders of the rebels.

A number of people who have become known for their goodness or heroism are from Essex. They include Captain Oates who is commemorated in Gestingthorpe church, Elizabeth Fry, the prison reformer, who is buried in the Quaker burial ground in Barking, and Doctor Barnado who worked in the East End and the deprived areas of south west Essex to save destitute children and founded his Girls Village home at Barkingside.

St. Mary's, Fryerning

Some Essex Stories

Canewdon and the witches

One village, Canewdon was always known for its witches. The stories go that it had six witches, three in silk and three in cotton and there had always been this number from time immemorial. It is rumoured that Canewdon always has had a cunning man who rules the witches and is believed to continue to do so still. Essex has always been a superstitious county and prone to a belief in witchcraft. Most Essex villages had a wise man or woman who could charm warts, help find lost things, tell fortunes, use herbal medicine and cast spells so girls might know who their sweetheart will be. This has not always been so harmless. In the 17th century Matthew Hopkins, the self styled Witch Finder General boasted that he had had sixty women hanged in one year. At that time, there was a genuine witch hunt in which a large number of old women were put to death, some legally by 'due process of law' using the ordeals of ducking and pricking for the dead spot where they were believed to feel no pain but, in a number of cases, old women were murdered through the malice or ignorance of their neighbours who denounced them as witches. As the number of superstitions I have listed testifies, Essex is a county where belief in magic and unofficial medicine remained strong until very recent times and can be said to influence many in their lives still.

Coggeshall jobs

Coggeshall has been known in Essex for the Coggeshall jobs, like the time the church clock struck thirteen and they put a hurdle across the road to stop the chime escaping; the man who found his ladder was too short so he cut a rung off the bottom to put on the top; when the town band, being told how nice their music sounded in the road, all downed instruments and went to listen and when two men having had a bit to drink, decided to move the church and they couldn't move it against the wind so they took off their jackets and went round the other side; when they came back their jackets had gone and they realised that they had pushed the church over them.

An old rhyme ran:

Braintree for the pure, and Bocking for the
poor;
Coggeshall for the jeering town and
Kelvedon for the whore.

Quite what Coggeshall and Kelvedon had done to deserve that reputation, no-one now knows but as, historically, Braintree was a centre for non-conformity and hence obvious goodness, this probably accounts for its purity.

The Peculiar People

The Peculiar People were an Essex based sect, originating from Rochford. The sect was quite common in South Essex and Dengie, where one of the last chapels remains at Tillingham. The word 'Peculiar' means a special set apart people, not odd or strange as in modern usage. They were what we would now call fundamentalists who believed in the literal meaning of the Bible; their services were conducted by the members of the congregation and lasted all day; they had no pastors. They would bring their food with them to be kept warm on the stove in winter. They did not believe in doctors and in earlier times were prosecuted for not seeking medical treatment for their children. They were known for their honesty and straightforward dealing - many were in trade.

The Black Dog in Marshland and other supernatural effects

In common with parts of Suffolk, a monstrous dog was rumoured to haunt the marsh road around Tollesbury and on Dengie. To see it was death. Prosaically, it is likely that the smugglers made sure that the dog roved the lanes when they were about their business to scare people into staying at home. Tiptree

Southend Pier -
the longest in Europe

Heath was a major centre for them and it is no coincidence that the legends of the black dog were strongest there.

Essex also has a number of other supernatural claims to fame - the most haunted house at Borley, Anne Boleyn haunts New Hall, the ghosts at St Osyth, the dragon at Wormingford, the ghostly Roman legions at Bradwell-juxta-Mare, marching to their fort at Othona and the hauntings at St Anne's Castle, the pub on the main road at Great Leighs.

The Dunmow Flitch

In Dunmow, there was an old custom which had died out in 1751 that if a couple could prove that they had never said a cross word to each other, nor had regretted their marriage, they were awarded a flitch of bacon. They had to kneel on pointed stones and take the following oath:

You shall swear by custom of confession
That you ne'er made marital transgression
Nor since you were married man and wife
By household brawls or contentious strife
Or otherwise at bed and board
Offended each other in deed or in word
Or since the parish clerk said amen
Wished yourselves unmarried again
Or in a twelvemonth and a day
Repented even in thought any way
But continued true in thought and desire
As when you joined hands in holy quire.

The successful claimants were carried round the town in the prior's chair, which is still kept in Little Dunmow church. The custom was revived last century and now takes the form of a trial with be-wigged judges and prosecutors and defenders. Incidentally, the first lifeboat is said to have been tested in the pond at Dunmow by Lionel Lukin.

The Whispering Court of Rochford

At midnight on the first Wednesday after Michaelmas, the stewards and tenants met and processed by torchlight to King's Hill to the whispering post in Rochford where the Chief

Steward of the Manor met them and in a whisper opened the proceedings of the manorial court by calling the roll. The tenants had to answer in a whisper and the business was recorded using a piece of charcoal. The whispering court lasted until the nineteenth century although it was revived briefly in the 1950s. It was a great opportunity for roistering and drunkenness and this may account for its cessation or supression.

The Essex sense of humour is mixed. It is subtle in words and broad in deed as some of the stories above suggest. Generally it is not usually malicious but it could be pointed if the butts of people's humour were thought to have got above themselves or had taken advantage unfairly.

C. H. Warren tells a story of the Essex love of the practical joke when a father and son, who were known to be near and crafty, had been taking wood from the woodpile on the farm. One day, their mates drilled some holes in the logs and filled them with gunpowder which they took home put on the fire and blew soot and heaven knows what down the chimney.

The old farm hand had been given a young lad from the next village to help him with some hedging. He was asked by the farmer to keep an eye on him and to start to 'larn he how to hedge'. He set the boy to work picking up the clippings and was explaining to him how to lay a hedge and why it was important to work steadily and to keep a watch out for birds nests so as not to worry the birds. The lad said but when can I have a go with the shears; the old man explained that he wasn't ready yet; they were dangerous; the boy kept on and eventually the old man was provoked to say "Stop yer clanjanderin do, there's plenty time boy. There's a hool day termorrer we ent started on yet".

The one thing Essex people love to do is to lead someone on to boast about themselves or to claim knowledge of something they know nothing about in public - best of all a foreigner in the pub - until they get out on a limb with some unbelievable story. The foreigner may never know that he has been taken down a peg but everyone else will.

People are remembered over generations for things they did - they become part of the folklore of a village. Often men are given nicknames which are hard to account for. In my own village I can recall two - Hommer Moss and Hastings Brazier. Why they got those names no-one can remember but they were always known that way and indeed most never knew their given names.

Essex men were known as Essex calves because of the livestock fattened on the marshes for the London market and contrariwise, a calf was known as an Essex lion.

St. Mary's Church, Maldon

Essex Curiosities, Sights and Wonders

The county has a number of sights, curiosities and wonders. Some are well known such as Finchingfield, one of the picture book villages, the great house at Audley End, Thaxted, Dedham and the Essex half of Constable Country, Epping and Hatfield Forests, Coggeshall and especially Paycockes as well as the seaside resorts of Southend, Clacton, Walton and Frinton, the latter having suffered the indignity of having a fish and chip shop, now seems likely to have a public house for the first time to blight its refinement.

There are however a lot of less well known but still impressive things to see in Essex. Some are unique; some are unusual and unexpected.

All Saints Maldon - the church has a very rare triangular tower to fit into the cramped site. The church is also notable for connections with the Washington family who were reported to have made good in America and there is a window from Maldon in the USA, as a memorial to Lawrence Washington who was George's great-grandfather and was also rector of Purleigh for 10 years).

Greensted - the oldest wooden church in England. It is likely that many churches in Essex originally looked like the nave of Greensted because wood was plentiful, there is no good building stone and brick making had not then been developed, although the Saxons certainly knew how to use bricks which they re-cycled from Roman buildings. There is some debate as to its actual age, some have claimed that it was a chapel built to house the remains of St. Edmund, the martyred king of East Anglia, and others have said that the timbers are not old enough to be Anglo-Saxon in origin but what ever the facts are, the Church is well worth going to see.

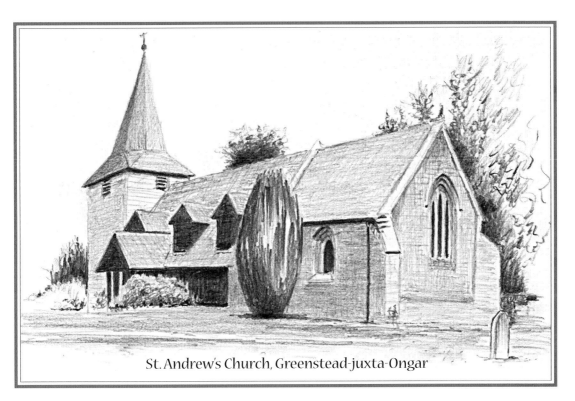

St. Andrew's Church, Greenstead-juxta-Ongar

The wooden towers of the churches - many of the churches of mid and south Essex have intricate wooden towers displaying great wood working skill; the most interesting are at Blackmore, West Hanningfield, Stock and Navestock.

The oldest use of brick - well to be honest, Essex and Suffolk compete here. The Anglo-Saxons used brick but apparently never made it. Brick making is recorded as again taking place in the 13th century at Little Coggeshall and Polstead just across the Stour in Suffolk. Which was first is now not clear. Essex made great use of brick in its church towers across the County and at Chignal Smealy, the whole church, including the font, is of brick. John Betjeman celebrated this in his description of Essex churches with brickwork red as a bonfire.

Copford Church paintings - here there is a complete set of Norman wall paintings which were restored in the 19th century but still give a unique idea of what a church looked like before the Protestant reformation in the 16th century. Of particular interest is the zodiac painted across the chancel arch - you might wonder what this has to do with Christianity.

Colchester is the oldest recorded town in Britain with a set of Roman walls, a Roman gate, the foundations of the temple of the Emperor Claudius (of I Claudius fame), the largest castle keep in the country, two ruined monasteries, the bullets in the walls of the Red Lion from the siege in the Civil War and jumbo. If you don't know what or who jumbo is, just ask someone in Colchester or look upwards.

Galleywood is reputed to have the only church inside a racecourse in the world. The racecourse has been defunct since before the Second World War although you can still see the course itself marked by the white railings but the grandstands have gone. The church is a twin of that at Widford. There were two brothers, the Pryors of Hylands, who decided to build churches at the neighbouring parishes in rivalry. Galleywood's spire is the more prominent as it stands high as a landmark in the Wid valley and can be seen for miles around.

Chelmsford is notable as the seat of the cathedral and it was the first town to be lit by electricity. It was the home of Cromptons who were responsible for many electrical innovations and for the installation of electric lights in some of the palaces of Europe but to all radio enthusiasts, its greater claim to fame is as the place where the first radio broadcasts were made and where Marconi set up the first factory to make radio equipment. Incidentally, the name of Writtle became famous nationally as it was part of the first call sign in public broadcasting in Britain. The site is in Mildmay Road and is marked with a blue plaque. It is not generally known that the first time that Stirling Moss and Fangio met was in Essex at the test track at Boreham.

Little Maplestead church has one of the six round naves in the country. The nearest of the others is at Cambridge. The manor was held by the Knights Templars who built their churches as replicas of the Church of the Holy Sepulchre in Jerusalem. They held a fair bit of land in Essex with the Temple Barns at Cressing being a very impressive reminder of their presence as well as an important part of the country's heritage of old wooden buildings

Saffron Walden is written of as being one of the most perfect small towns in the East of England. The church, the host of old buildings and its mediaeval streets make it a joy to walk around. There are two special features which make a visit worthwhile - the maze and the number of pargetted buildings, including the Essex giant.

The town museum has some interesting exhibits, including a piece of human skin allegedly from a Danish raider who was caught, flayed, and his skin nailed to the church door at Hadstock, whether as a simple punishment or to deter others from raiding is unknown but, if the latter then the continuing Danish raids suggests it had little effect. The town takes its name from the saffron crocus which gave it prosperity in earlier days but it is no longer grown as a cash crop locally despite its reputation as being worth more per ounce than gold.

The Viper, Mill Green

Layer Marney Tower lies in the unfrequented country between Tiptree and Colchester. It is quite simply an enormous Tudor gatehouse which, had the rest of the building been finished, would have been part of one of the most spectacular mansions in the country.

At Rivenhall the church has been recently excavated and evidence of a Roman villa found under it with a clear Christian connection. In addition in a Victorian restoration with some ugly concrete rendering, the Anglo-Saxon walls of the church have been found in a good state of repair. The Church is also worth visiting for some impressive stained glass brought from France by a Victorian rector.

Pleshey in remote mid Essex has the remains of a large scale fortification. Its name means just that from the French plessis. The village is celebrated by Shakespeare in Richard the Second:

… Bid him - ah what?
With all good speed at Plashy visit me,
Alack, and what shall good old York there see,
But empty lodgings and unfurnish'd walls,
Unpeopled offices, untrodden stones,
And what hear there for welcome but my groans?

Like Great Canfield, a few miles west, Pleshey is more celebrated for what glory has departed rather than what remains so the atmosphere in both villages is evocative of a vanished feudal past.

The Anglo-Saxon doors at Hadstock and Buttsbury. The churches in these villages have the two oldest doors in the country. The one at Hadstock is probably in the door it was made for; that at Buttsbury has been moved after the church was rebuilt.

Essex has the only pub in the country named solely after a snake - the Viper at Mill Green, near Ingatestone.

An interesting coincidence is that one day
Chelmsford's roof and Writtle steeple
Fell down one day and killed no people
This was in January, 1800. It might have been a forerunner of the great Essex earthquake of 1882 which devastated much of the area south of Colchester.

Essex Food

It has to be said that Essex does not lead the country in the elegance, sophistication and delicacy of its traditional food. The raw materials are good and Essex gardeners are proud of the vegetables they produce. These include Colchester oysters (the best in the country whatever foreigners from South of the Thames might say), Tiptree strawberries and strawberry jam, cockles from Leigh on Sea, Tolleshunt D'Arcy Spice apples but cheeses are not produced any more, there are no good hams, no indigenous turkeys; even saffron is no longer grown. Essex does produce what many cooks consider to be the best salt from Maldon. The food of the people however was a reflection of the poverty of the country until quite recent times.

Essex cheeses were notorious. I found this verse written by John Skelton in John Pusey's Discovery of Old Essex:

A caudle of Essex cheese
Was well a foot thick
Full of maggots quick
It was huge and great
And mighty strong meat
For the devil to eat
It was tart and pungente.

Essex, like the other eastern counties, was a boiling county - meat, vegetables and especially suet for dumplings and puddings. Dinner for children was often a suet pudding served up with gravy (saace) followed by boiled vegetables and maybe another suet pudding for afters with a spoon of jam.

Here is a recipe (or a receipt from old Essex) for a bacon and onion pudding:

8 oz/200g self raising flour
4oz/100g suet
3oz/75g smoked streaky bacon
1 medium onion
Salt
10-12 tablespoons or 15ml of water

Put a large pan of water on to boil. Cut up the bacon and onion into small pieces. Put the flour, suet and salt into a mixing bowl and mix thoroughly. Add the water until the mix becomes sticky to the touch, then add the bacon and onion and stir in until they are evenly distributed throughout.

Put the mixture into a pre-greased basin and cover with greaseproof paper and a pudding cloth or a lid, put in the pan of boiling water, reduce the heat and let it simmer for about $1\frac{1}{4}$ to $1\frac{1}{2}$ hours. Make sure that the pan does not boil dry. Serve hot with a choice of vegetables from the garden.

It could be made economically with a few bits of bacon and more onion but nowadays, it would have a good content of meat and vegetable.

Traditionally, rook pie was a delicacy in some parts. The backbone of the rooks had to be removed or the meat was reported to be unpleasant to taste. Most traditional Essex food goes back to poverty with making the best of very little and meagre scrapings having to do. The man of the family would get whatever meat was going. Rabbit was rarely eaten because in the old days it was the preserve of the farmer or the quality and they punished poaching with all the severity they could muster. Since they or their friends served on the bench, you can imagine that few of those caught ever escaped justice which was twice visited on the family if the man of the house was jailed.

In contrast to the food, Essex beer has always been good and remains so. Some of the best beer in the country is brewed at Hartford End by Ridleys who have been there since 1842. The other old county breweries have gone, even the massive Ind Coope works at Romford and, although Grays have kept their pubs, the brewery is now smart shops in Chelmsford. In compensation there are some small local firms brewing beer, most notably Crouch Vale at South Woodham (Ferrers) which owns two pubs at Stow Maries and Tillingham. Essex people also brewed, if that's the word, home-made wine in great quantities from anything that would ferment - pea pods, beet, potatoes, parsnips, wheat, paigles - are all examples of what you might be offered if someone said "Ha a glass of my woine mate. That'll do yer good."

George had moved from his beloved Essex to live his later years with his daughter in Norwich.. He fell ill and it soon became clear that he did not have long to go. The family gathered round his bed."

What can we do for you?" they asked old George.

"Tha only thing that'll dew me any good is a whiff of Essex air" whispered the old man.

"Dunt yew fret" said son-in-law Charlie, "I'll see to that". Next day he cycled from Norwich down to Maldon, when he arrived he let the air out of his tyres and pumped them up again and headed back to Norwich. Opening the front door he took the bike inside and carried it up the stairs. "You'll soon be alright George, here comes boy Charlie."

Charlie bent down unscrewed the valve and let all the air out of the tyre. Old George took one whiff - and passed away. "Oh dear!" exclaimed his daughter, "I had thought that would do him good." "Well," replied Charlie "I suppose that would have done if I hent a got that puncture in Stowmarket!"

Section Three

A Dictionary of
Essex Dialect

Shortly after his arrival in a new country parish, the vicar was asked to conduct a funeral service.

He announced: "I am very sorry that I cannot pay tribute to the deceased as I did not know him. But if any of you would like to say a few words, please feel free to do so."

There was complete silence in the little village church. The vicar tried again.

"Now please do not be shy, I'm sure someone would like to say a kindly word about our dear departed friend."

Another long silence. Suddenly, a voice from the back muttered:

"His bruther wus wuss!"

A Dictionary of Essex Dialect

A

Abroad - out/outdoors

Acrost - across

Acrost - to annoy someone - "You'll get acrost her (she) do you keep on so".

Adders meat - Field Horsetail

Afeard - afraid

Afters - pudding, sweet

Agin - against or next as in I left that spade agin the wall

Agure - fever. This was the ague, probably malaria, prevalent on the Essex marshes to which all the native born marshlanders were immune. In the old graveyards in the marshes you can see the short lives of the women (who often came from up country) and their children

Allow - accept/recognise as in "I allow that might be right".

Amuck - wrong

Arse - the bottom, back end as in "the arse hanging out uv his trouseys".

Arse-uppards - upside down

Arsy-tarsy - muddled

Arsy-varsy - upside down

Arter - after

Arternoon - afternoon

Arth - earth as in "Niver set yer seeds til you cin bare your backside in the arth".

Atomy - body

Atween - between

Atwixt - between

Awkard - awkward

B

Baingy - drizzly day

Bait - basket

Bait - food

Bandie - to mess about

Bandy - to argue - bandy words with

Bangers - breasts

Barmy - mad or daft

Barn yard - yard next to the barn

Basket - bastard

Bastatious - bad, mean - "A bastatious person"

Bate - temper

Batty - daft, mad

Bay - the space between the beams in a barn. This can be seen to great advantage in the Temple Barns at Cressing

Beast - animals usually cattle

Beer - mild ale

Behounced - dolled up to the nines

Belly-wanty - girth strap

Best - a useful expression - "best we do" meaning "it would be best if…".

Bevver/beaver/bever - elevenses

Bewley - wrong

Bezzle - guzzle

Billy Wix - owl

Bin - been as in "Where yer bin then?"

Blab - to talk loosely, to give away a secret.

Blabbermouth - someone who cannot hold their tongue

Blame - a mild curse

Blare - usually an animal moaning/making a lot of noise and fuss

Blast - a general word sometimes as a curse, sometimes as a means of emphasis - "Blast that snew grub at her wedding do."

Blazes - in a hurry

Blazes - hell - "go to blazes"

Billy Wix

Blessed - a mild curse or term of abuse for a child being a nuisance " That blessed boy has riled me all day."

Blind - blossom that did not fruit

Blind worm - slow worm

Blinkin - very as in "Blinkin stoopid"

Blob - blunt ended

Bluster - to boast

Bodge - hasty, poor work. "I wouldn't use he for your job mate do, he'll bodge it"

Bobbing Joan - bulrush

Bogged - marshy

Bonka - fine young girl

Bonker - big/well built

Bonkers - mad

Bor - used when two or more men met - "How are you bor?"

Boy - pronounced booey, a boy, but also used when talking of men in general - the old boys. This and bor are often confused by foreigners.

Bobbing Joan

Brackly - brittle

Bran noo - new/unused

Bread and Cheese - new hawthorn shoots

Bread and pullit - the invariable answer when a child asked what was for tea or dinner

Break up - the end of term at school. There was an old rhyme in my village which we used to chant going home on the last day of term:

"No more school
No more stick
No more nasty ol rithmetic"

Brimming - full

Brown Sugar - slush, which bigger kids pushed down the necks of smaller children

Brush - trim a hedge

Brush - fox tail

Brush off - to ignore

Bugger - a slightly indelicate word used by both men and women (although not always in front of each other). It is frequently used in Essex speech. It has a variety of meanings such as:-

bugger off - to go away or as a means of expressing disbelief;

bugger that - no I don't like that or I am not doing that;

little owd bugger - a term of affection for a boy.

Buggery - a strong negative as in "Will I buggery". It also means going at top speed - "Cor I sin him humpin along like buggery".

Buggied - maggots in fruit

Bumble footed - game legged/one leg longer than the other

Bumby hole - ash pit/sewage pit

Bung - throw

Bunkum - rubbish

Bunk up - sexual congress

Bush - a splinter

Butcher Bird - shrike

Butter harsey - a light red haw

Buzz - to hurry around busy to little effect. "Well I sin her buzz around but she don't do nothin for all that"

Buzz off - go away

C

Cack handed - clumsy

Cackle - noisy people talking; also a hen after laying an egg

Cad - last pig of the litter

Caddle - muddle/rush/state

Call - need. "There ent ner call to talk like that here mate."

Canker - rose hip/field poppy

Cards - dominoes

Catching - contagious

Causey - a causeway

Cawfin - coffin

Chance child - illegitimate

Chap - derogatory term for someone who has got above himself - "What a fine chap he is in his best trouseys on a Sunday off to the pub".

Charlock - (also carlock) camomile

Chase - the lane/track to a farm

Chat - whitethroat

Chipper - pleased with yourself

Chuffed - pleased

Chuffer - steam engine/traction engine

Clamjammerin/clanjanderin - gossiping, talkative

Clamp - a way of storing potatoes and root crops

Clip - to hit someone, usually a difficult child - "I'll clip your ears mate"

Clodhopper - awkward, clumsy person

Poppy

Clout - to hit hard

Clump - to hit

Clunchy - thick set, stocky

Coax - stroke a dog

Cock-eyed - askew, bent, twisted, out of line

Company - visitors

Concrate - concrete/cement

Contrary - difficult, awkward tempered

Cop - both to throw something gently and to get hit hard by something "He copped the lot right in his face"

Cor - all purpose introduction to an exclamation - "Cor boy, you ent half headin for a clout"

Cosset - smallest pig

Cosset - make a fuss of

Crabbin - to fish for crabs using worms or offal

Crake - to gloat or boast. "He ent got nawthin to crake on. I knew he when his arse was out of his trouseys."

Crankled - twisted/winding

Creechur - creature

Crick - strained, twisted

Crows claw - corn crow foot

Cruel - badly - me knees hurt something cruel

Crump - a circular enclosure

Culch - grass

Curse of Cromwell - ragwort

Cuss - to curse as in "I don't give a tinker's cuss what you think"

D

Dag - dew/ wet ground

Damfi - damned as in "Damfi noo" (Damned if I know)

Dank - dew, wet weather

Dare say - used to give some authority to a statement - " I dare say that she might be coming home directly."

Daresent - dare not

Devil Bird

Deadified - tired out, dead beat.

Deal - a lot of something as in a good deal of

Devil bird - the swift

Devil dodger - someone who switched between church and chapel

Devils guts - bindweed

Dibble - a stick, often a broken spade handle, for making holes for planting out

Dickey - donkey

Dickey - unwell

Diddy - small

Die kind - die easily

Dike - privy

Ding - to box or rattle the ears

Dinkey - donkey

Dinkey - small and neat

Dint - did not

Directly - an elastic term meaning from here to eternity - see the section on Essex and time

Divvy - not very bright, stupid

Doddle - pull

Doddle - something easy and quick to do

Doddy - small

Dodman also hodmedod - a snail

Dogs - feet - "Me dogs are barkin" meaning my feet ache

Dollop - a big portion

Dollops - great lazy woman

Dolly - washing stick

Dolour - suffer/pain (pronounced duller)

Don't ought/didn't ought - ought not

Don't think - a positive statement - an emphasis as in "he's a right one I don't think."

Dop - curtsey

Doubt - suspect/believe

Dow - dove

Ducks and drakes - skimming stones on a pond or still water

Dunnekin - privy (maybe the origin of the Australian word dunnee)

E

Earnest - Hiring money for servants and farm staff

Elbow grease - effort, hard work

Elevenses - the mid morning break for food

Ellum - the elm tree

Ent - aren't/haven't

Ent half - very probably

Everlastin - continuing; often as in "she is everlastin botherin me for money".

F

Fair to middlin - feeling fit and well, usually in response to "How do yer dew?"

Fairy rings - rings made in grass by toadstools or other fungus

Dodman (or Hodmedod)

Fall - a woman will fall and become pregnant

Fancy Man - boy friend, inevitably, of a married woman. I can recall coming in and catching the end of some gossip between my mother and a friend which was "She may have a fancy man or two on the go but Eva's very particular at home." I was never sure whether this was damning with faint praise or praising with faint damns; it could have been a charitable attempt to find good, of course.

Fare - go or do - "I fare to see that"

Farrow - litter of pigs

Fartarsin - meddling/messing around

Fast and loose - to cheat someone, to take an unfair advantage.

Favour - take after (resemble), prefer

Feed - grass pasture

Felfet - missle thrush

Fetch up - falter, stop against

Fetch up - be sick

Few/Foo - an indefinite number from two upwards depending on the circumstances

Finnicky - painstaking, fussy

Five finger - oxlip

Flat - sad, or unrisen bread and cake

Fleet - shallow rooted

Foreign - not local - anywhere from the next village to the ends of the earth

Form - the place where a hare sits, often where it brings up its young

Fourses - afternoon break

Frackshus - quarrelsome, difficult

Frank hern - a heron

Frit - frightened

Fruz - frozen, cold

Fumble fisted - clumsy, cack handed

Furze - gorse

Fust - first

Fusty - stale smelling

G

Gal/gel - a girl of any age; often used as a prefix as in Gal Ruby

Gammicking - gossip

Gawp/gawk/garp - to stare rudely at something or someone, "What are yer gawpin at gal?"

Gays - pictures/photographs in newspapers

Gazunder - chamber pot

Genteel - kind

Ginst - near

Glouted - stared

Gob - mouth

Gob - a lump of food

Gob - to spit

Gobbler - a turkey

Goffle - to wolf food down

Good few - quite a lot

Good-un - good person/woman also "He was cussin like a good-un"

Goos-gog - gooseberry

Gowd - gold

Grey rock - rock dove

Grizzle guts - a moaner or complainer

Grouts - tea or coffee strainings

Grumpy - tetchy, ill tempered

Guts - insides

Gutter - drain

H

Haft - wooden handle of a tool

Hain - raise

Hainish - snobbish

Hang - the fruit on a tree or bush "That's a good hang o apples yer got there".

Hansel - an advance on pay or payment

Harsey - a haw

Goos-gogs

Hatch - door fastener

Haulms - stems left after harvesting/stubble

Have - used instead of has

Hawking - clearing the throat and spitting

He - used as in - "My mate, he say .."

Headest - cleverest

Headland - area on the side of a field jutting out

Heave - throw, originally sheaves but now a general word

Hedge betty - hedge sparrow

Hedge hopper - gypsy

Hens (hins) - always used instead of chickens

Highful - proud/snobbish

Holler - shouting and bawling

Horkey - harvest

Horn owl - long eared owl

Horseman - carter

Housen - houses

Hoverer - kestrel

Howd - hold - as in "Howd ye hard there".

Hum - smell/stink

Hump - to go along at speed

Hump - sexual congress

Humpy - hump backed

Hunk - a large lump as in a hunk o bread

Hunks - disagreeable old person

I

I never - the all purpose denial for children

Imitate - pretend

Ind - the end, usually to stop an argument - "That's an ind of it".

Innards - guts etc.

J

Jahney - a day's work

Jar - annoy

Jasper - a wasp

Jeremiah

Jereboam/Jeremiah/Jerry - chamber pot

Jib - restless

Jigger - person, man

Jip - pain and discomfort

Jollifications - celebration, a party.

Jollop - liquid - sometimes medicinal

Jonnick/Jonnock - straightforward

Judder - shake about, rattle

Junket - over lavish festivity, usually at public expense

K

Keys - ash seeds

Kilter - straight or repair

Kinda - sort

Knoll - small hill with a flat top

L

Lagsome - muddy

Largess - money paid at harvest to the reapers

Larn - teach as in "I larned he how ter do that"

Larrup - to beat

Lather - to beat

Lather - sweat

Lay - state or reckon - "I lay that'll rain come morning".

Lickerty split - jumping up quickly, rush off

Liefer - rather

Linen line - clothes line

Lollop - rolling along

Long tailed rabbit - pheasant

Looker - foreman/overseer

Lord - the leader of the harvest mowers now overtaken by mechanisation

Lords and Ladies - wild arum

M

Maggetty - ill tempered

Maggot - a bee in the bonnet, an obsession

Make tea - brew tea

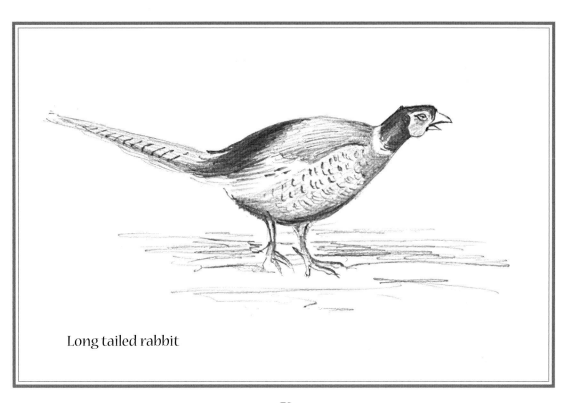

Long tailed rabbit

Nanny Washtail

Mammuck - to gobble food

Manger - a feed trough

Mate - an all purpose term of familiarity used of and by both sexes

Matter - pus etc. from a wound

Mawkin - a scarecrow

Maze - to confuse, befuddle

Meads - water meadows

Meece - mice

Mend - sort something out, fix, "That'll mend it"

Midda/Midder - meadow

Mine - my house - "we'll go round mine for a cup of tea if you like"

Mizzle - drizzle, light rain

Moither or mither - worry

Moocher - lazy loafer

Morge - a miry bit of soil

Morper - Hedge sparrow

Mosie - dawdle along

Muck - animal waste - in refined usage

My Godfathers - mild blasphemy - "My Godfathers child, what hev yew done now then?"

N

Nanny washtail - wagtail

Native - born here

Natural - simple, educationally challenged

Nice as pie - pleasant or alternatively two faced

Ninny - a fool or an idiot

Nucular - nuclear as in power station

Nutten - nothing

O

Obstinacious - obstinate

Ockud - awkward

Off of - from

Oil - paraffin

Old Man's Nightcap

Old harry - curlew
Old man's nightcap - bindweed
Ollus/allus - always
On the drag - late
Opputary - quarrelsome
Ours - our house
Oven - cooker
Owd - old, but it is not always used in relation to age but as a term of endearment and sometimes frustration.

P

Paigles - cowslips
Palm - pussy willow
Pancakes - cowpats
Parky - cold
Particular - clean, house-proud, careful
Pea shucks - pea pods
Peck - pick

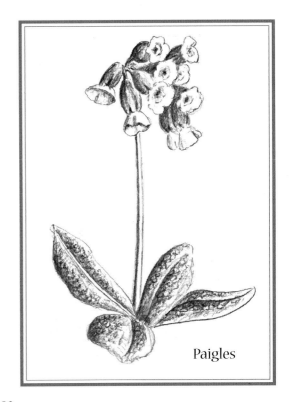

Paigles

Pezzicking - bustling
Pig muddle - in trouble
Pingle - play with food at the table
Pin cushion - scabious
Pitch - perch
Plum Pudding - red campion
Poke - a small bag
Poor man's weather glass - scarlet pimpernel
Privy - outside toilet
Proper - very good
Proper - decent/seemly
Proper - very, as in proper poorly
Pudding poke - long-tailed tit
Pus/puss - a purse
Pussy footing - dithering, dabbling

Q

Quackle - choke
Quite a few - a lot of

R

Rain bird - green woodpecker
Rainbow ploughing - a technique of curved ploughing parallel with the hedgerows
Rake - a lot of
Rattle along - go fast
Receipt - recipe
Reckon - believe, think
Regular - very much
Reis - haulm of peas or beans; this is local to north Essex
Rile - annoy
Roaring - a child's bawling or crying; occasionally also used of a donkey
Rot gut - poor thin beer
Rum - odd
Run - neglected (of land) -"he let that land run".

S

Saace - gravy or vegetables with food, also cheek from a child.

Scan - read

Scrapping - hurrying to finish something

Screws - arthritis/rheumatism

Scrotch - a v shaped twig for a catapult

Seemly - decent

Several - an indefinite number from two upwards depending on the circumstances

Shanty - a shack or poorly built house

Shires/sheers - anywhere outside the Eastern counties; usually it was spoken as a term of disapproval

Shirt buttons - stitchwort

Short-waisted - bad tempered

Shrimpled - wrinkled

Shucks - shell peas/ pea pods

Shuv - shove, push

Shuv off - go away

Shy - secret

Skint - hard up, broke

Skip or skep - a basket

Sling - throw

Sliver - thin slice/splinter

Slud - sludgy mud

Snaffle - pilfer, steal by finding

Snathe - scythe handle

Snew - snowed

Snob - cobbler/shoemaker

Soels - time of day. "I gave him the soels of the day". This is not used now but it has been recorded in the last fifty or so years and is directly related to the old English soel, meaning season.

Spiffin - good

Spiffler - fusspot

Spittin - few drops of rain

The "Splash" at Little Baddow

Spitty - house sparrow
Splash - ford
Sprindles - hazel rods
Springles - hazel rods - north Essex term in thatching
Spud - a farmer's stick
Squirt - mouthy young lad
Squit - disagreeable little person
Stackyard - main yard on a farm
Starchy - starling
Star naked - stark naked
Stingy - bitter, cold of the wind
Stuff - all purpose word for things
Suckers - sweets
Swift - a newt

T

Taint - it is not
Tares - weeds

Taters - potatoes
Teemin - pouring with rain
Tempering - mixing, often mortar
Tetchy - peevish
Then - this is very often added to questions - "What are you a-doing that for there then?" - but has no meaning as such
Thingumey - used when a speaker has forgotten the name of someone
Thingymebob - something the name of which has escaped the speaker
Thraving - stacking sheaves to dry
Thumping - big/huge
Thumping - bad as in a headache
Ticker - heart
Tiddly wink - wagtail
Tiddy - small
Tidy - a lot
Tidy few - quite a lot
Tig tig - call for pigs

Taters

Time/times - while

Tine - prong

Tissick - dry cough

Tits - cows' udders

To - close as in put the door to

Toffee nosed - haughty, snobbish

Top top - call to move an animal along

Totty bag - bag tied round the waist for gleaning

Traipse - trudge

Tramways - tractor etc. lines in a field

Trouseys - trousers

Trunky - nosey

Tumble - farm cart

Tumbril - farm cart

Twisty - fretful (of a child)

Twit - a fool and to tease

Twitch - couch grass

Twizzle - twisted

U

Ull - will

Un - one as in little un

Unloose - untie

Unt - won't

Up-ind - turn over, stand on end

Upshot - outcome

W

Wain - wagon

Wantz - crossroads

Weskit - waistcoat

Whatsisname - a general term for either a person or an object

Whatsit - something of which the speaker has forgotten the name

Whinnick - whine

Whodyermeflick - Whats-his-name

Wholly - very

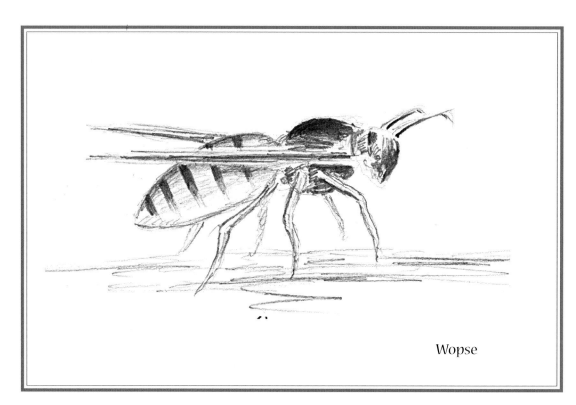

Wopse

Woite - white

Wonderful - very

Wopse - wasp

Worry guts - moaner, worrier

Worsent - worse

Wrong - angry/cross "I should hold your tongue mate, don't you'll git her wrong."

Wuss - worse

Y

Yard - back garden

Yattering - talkative

Yit - yet

Yourne - yours

Yours - your house

Z

Zackly - Exactly - "I told her zackly what I thought of she".

On reaching the age of 80 an Essex maiden aunt turned her thoughts to making arrangements for her demise. "I hent bin berholden ter enyone in my life and I ent a gornta start now," she mused.

She went along to the undertakers to make arrangements for her funeral and she was invited to select the lining material for her coffin. The undertaker said:"We normally bury the married women with a deep purple lining, but unmarried women like yourself usually have a nice piece of white taffeta."

The old dear thought for a moment. "Tell you what" she eventually replied, "Yew kin use the white tafeter but kin yew trim tha edges with papple jist ter let 'em know I hed my moments!"

Books and References

Essex has some literary background, although there are no great masterpieces written by Essex authors equivalent to Thomas Hardy's Wessex novels. S. L. Bensusan wrote a series of short stories about the people of Marshland - Dengie - from 1910 to the 1950s and his stories of poachers, farmers, farm hands and carters whose country wisdom was pitted against rich farmers, the gentry and furriners from the sheers which might deserve reviving. His portrait of a wise woman is particularly worth reading. There is one great classic by Sabine Baring-Gould who was rector of East Mersea. He wrote Mehalah, a romance of the marshlands which deals with the story of a woman's love which comes to a tragic ending (for her). Although it is often cited as an important book for the county, I doubt that it is read much, if at all, these days. Harrison Ainsworth, a high Victorian novelist, wrote about the Dunmow Flitch and Dick Turpin who was an Essex man from Hempstead; he is censured by the slightly pompous for romanticising a common criminal. More recently, many of Margery Allingham's detective stories have an Essex background - especially Mystery Mile - although she did portray the county as Suffolk in some.

Of books about Essex, C. H. Warren has written a portrait of the county as it was just after the War as well as a portrait of Great Samford where he lived. Spike Mays' books Five Miles from Bunkum and Reuben's Corner depict Ashdon in North Essex most eloquently. Stan Jarvis has written a number of books on Essex, most recently about Essex Privies, all of which will repay reading and I have previously mentioned John Pusey's book, the Discovery of Old Essex. John Betjeman knew and loved Essex. He often stayed at the Green

Man at Little Braxted and his poem on Essex which I have quoted shows his appreciation of the County. His description of Essex churches in the Collins Guide to English Parish Churches is worth reading. Finally, Norman Scarfe's Shell Guide to Essex is a very good introduction to the architecture of Essex, but perhaps, more as the title suggests, he puts the building in the context of the landscape or the surrounding town or village rather than, as in Pevsner's Buildings of Essex (now sadly very much in need of updating), providing a catalogue of descriptions of notable buildings. He is understandably and justifiably rude about official recent, modern day vandalism in the towns, especially Chelmsford.

Conclusion

This short book has picked up a few of the old country words which are still around. Many have gone out of use with the coming of the farm machinery that would do the work of ten men and the movement of the men from the land into the factories and other work. Many more have disappeared through the spread of modern communication and most of all through television. It is important that we try to retain what we can of these words because they reflect the people who used them, who invented new words for new things and who kept the memory of the country back to the times that their ancestors started to arrive in Essex more than fifteen hundred years ago. I argue that the dialects of these islands are as much a part of the heritage as the buildings and the landscape. Indeed the landscape we see in the county was made by the people who spoke the Essex dialect and who lie in the churchyards and in the war cemeteries in France and Belgium, forgotten for the most part.

The old dialect and the spoken English it represented did go right back to those old times and a few words still survive in common speech. This brings us back to larn, which as I said at the start is still used in Essex in its old sense of teach and I hope that you might have learned a little (in the modern sense) about the Essex dialect and those who spoke it and perhaps something about a county which has been much maligned in recent years.

An Ending

This is the land that the sea mists muffle
This is the land where the marsh creeks fill
Green lit dawns that the black wings ruffle
Smoke red tides where the sunsets spill

This is the land where the farmsteads muster
Field on field till the sky sweeps down
Where the bold earth lies bare to the bold winds bluster
And the trees sing shrill on the hills low crown

These are the names for the tongue's rich savour
Stapleford Tawney and Tolleshunt Knights
Margaret Roding and Magdalen Laver
High Easter and Hainault and such delights

This is my home
The place I love.

Ancient Tree
Stump,
Hatfield
Forest

Other recent titles from NOSTALGIA Publications

THE HOBBIES STORY
Terry Davy
Over 100 years of the history of a well known fretwork and engineering company

MEMORIES OF NORFOLK CRICKET
Philip Yaxley
200 years of history of Norfolk Cricket

LARN YARSELF NORFOLK
Keith Skipper
A comprehensive guide to the Norfolk dialect

RUSTIC REVELS
Keith Skipper
Humorous country tales and cartoons

LARN YARSELF SILLY SUFFOLK
David Woodward
A comprehensive guide to the Suffolk dialect

THASS A RUM OW JOB
Tony Clarke
More Tales of Tha Boy Jimma

KID'S PRANKS AND CAPERS
Frank Reed
Nostalgic recollections of childhood

LARN YERSALF NORTHAMPTONSHIRE DIALECT
Mia Butler and Colin Eaton
A guide to the Northamptonshire dialect